The White Lie

OTHER BOOKS BY DON PATERSON

Nil Nil
God's Gift to Women
The Eyes

The White Lie

New and Selected Poetry

DON PATERSON

Graywolf Press
SAINT PAUL, MINNESOTA

Publication of this volume is made possible in part by a grant provided by the Minnesota State Arts Board through an appropriation by the Minnesota State Legislature, and by a grant from the National Endowment for the Arts. Significant support has also been provided by the Bush Foundation; Dayton's Project Imagine with support from Target Foundation; the McKnight Foundation; a grant made on behalf of the Stargazer Foundation; and other generous contributions from foundations, corporations, and individuals. To these organizations and individuals we offer our heartfelt thanks.

Published by Graywolf Press
2402 University Avenue, Suite 203
Saint Paul, Minnesota 55114
All rights reserved.

www.graywolfpress.org

Published in the United States of America
Printed in Canada

ISBN 1-55597-353-1

2 4 6 8 9 7 5 3 1
First Graywolf Printing, 2001

Library of Congress Control Number: 2001088663

Cover design: Julie Metz

Contents

Nil Nil

The Ferryman's Arms

About to sit down with my half-pint of Guinness
I was magnetized by a remote phosphorescence
and drawn, like a moth, to the darkened back room
where a pool-table hummed to itself in the corner.
With ten minutes to kill and the whole place deserted
I took myself on for the hell of it. Slotting
a coin in the tongue, I looked round for a cue—
while I stood with my back turned, the balls were deposited
with an abrupt intestinal rumble; a striplight
batted awake in its dusty green cowl.
When I set down the cue-ball inside the parched D
it clacked on the slate; the nap was so threadbare
I could screw back the globe, given somewhere to stand—
as physics itself becomes something negotiable
a rash of small miracles covers the shortfall:
I went on to make an immaculate clearance.
A low punch with a wee dab of side, and the black
did the vanishing trick while the white stopped
before gently rolling back as if nothing had happened,
shouldering its way through the unpotted colours.

The boat chugged up to the little stone jetty
without breaking the skin of the water, stretching,
as black as my stout, from somewhere unspeakable
to here, where the foaming lip mussitates endlessly,
trying, with a nutter's persistence, to read
and re-read the shoreline. I got aboard early,
remembering the ferry would leave on the hour
even for only my losing opponent;
but I left him there, stuck in his tent of light, sullenly
knocking the balls in, for practice, for next time.

Morning Prayer

after Rimbaud

I spend my life sitting, like an angel at the barber's,
with a mug in one hand, fag in the other,
my froth-slabbered face in the gantry mirror
while the smoke towels me down, warm and white.

On the midden of desire, the old dreams
still hold their heat, ferment, gently ignite—
once, my heart had thrown its weight behind them
but it saps itself now, stews in its own juice.

Having stomached my thoughts like a horrible linctus
—swilled down with, oh, fifteen, twenty pints—
I am roused only by the most bitter necessities:

then, the air high with the smell of opened cedar,
I pish gloriously into the dawn skies
while below me, the spattered ferns nod their assent.

Filter

Thrown out in a glittering arc
    as clear as the winterbourne,
the jug of Murphy's I threw back
    goes hissing off the stone.

Whatever I do with all the black
    is my business alone.

Exeunt

(i)
DROP SERENE

He poured the warm, clear guck into the mould
in which he'd already composed, with tweezers,
dead wasps on an everlasting flower
or ants filing over a leaf. When it was cold
he slaved at the surface, softening the camber
till it sat with the row of blebs on his mantelpiece,
each with its sequestered populace
like a hiccup in history, scooped out of amber.

As if it might stall the invisible cursor
drawing a blind down each page of his almanac
or the blank wall of water that always kept pace,
glittering an inch, half an inch from his back.
He was out in the garden, digging the borders
when it caught him, in a naturalistic pose.

(ii)
CURTAINS

You stop at the tourist office in Aubeterre,
a columbarium of files and dockets.
She explains, while you flip through the little leaflets
about the chapel and the puppet-theatre,
that everything is boarded up till spring,
including—before you can ask—the only hotel.
A moped purrs through the unbroken drizzle.
You catch yourself checking her hands for rings.

She prepares a light supper; you chat,
her fussy diction placing words in air
like ice in water. She leads you to her room
but gets the shivers while you strip her bare;
lifting her head, you watch her pupils bloom
into the whole blue iris, then the white.

(iii)
BIRD

The wind baffled lightly as they filled the grave
and a queasy flutter left us, the last faint
ripple of the peristaltic wave
that ushered her out. In eight months, her complaint
had whittled her down to the palsied sylph
who filched the car-keys from her snoring spouse
and went out to prove a point; then found herself,
like Alice, on the wrong side of the glass.

Later, back at the house, I overheard
the disembodied voices in the hall
where George, who'd only last another year,
was trying to be philosophical:
*Ach, there was nothin' o' her. She was nae mair
than a sparra, nae mair than a wee bird.*

(iv)

THE ELECTRIC BRAE

For three days and three nights, he has listened
to the pounding of a terrible jug band
now reduced to a wheezy concertina
and the disinterested thump of a tea-chest bass.
It seems safe to look: wires trail on the pillowcase,
a drip swings overhead; then the clear tent
becomes his father's clapped-out Morris Minor,
rattling towards home. The windscreen presents
the unshattered myth of a Scottish spring;
with discreet complicity, the road
swerves to avoid the solitary cloud.
On an easy slope, his father lets the engine
cough into silence. Everything is still.
He frees the brake: the car surges uphill.

Sunset, Visingsö

after Jørn-Erik Berglund

The lake has simplified
to one sleep-wave
bounced between shores.

All evening,
as superstition requires,
my eyes have not left it—

the fabulous animal
I will flay for the colour
its skin grows when it dreams.

Ezekiel

(i)

He was struggling down the ladder between decks,
his free arm lightly cradling the compass
like a great egg; he was sure he felt a pluck
at his chest, swaying above the last rung.
Imagining the ship about to rock
he leant to compensate: the compass stung
like a mule. They found him there, unconscious,
the gyro beside him, purring in its box.

The men from the university assemble
in a toolshed on a bleak Dundee estate,
politely clearing their throats while he unveils
the squat and massive tree of gyroscopes
and builds a rough chord on it, till the rumble
focuses to a pure hum. The coughing stops:
he has unlocked the hammer within the anvil.
It drills on his workbench, begins to levitate.

(ii)

The news of our approach had crossed the nation
entirely, so it seemed, by word of mouth—
a vast network so sensitively primed
that by the time we rolled up in the hired Toyota
the Three Professors of Music from Oxford University
had long secured their place in local myth.
Eager to help us with our dissertation
they had already booked the venue, fixed the time.

All time is lost in the music, and the drained jug.
When it returns, it catches at us like a ripcord—
the skipped beat from reel to jig—
instantaneously, the ring of dancers blur,
resolving as a wheel within a wheel,
a flashing zoetrope, rims full of eyes.
At the point the tune turns back to bite its tail
they pause, then stamp the floor from under us.

Sisters

for Eva

Back then, our well of tenements
powered the black torch that could find
the moon at midday: four hours later
the stars would be squandered on us.

❧

As the sun spread on her freckled back
I felt as if I'd turned the corner
to a bright street, scattered with coins;
for weeks, I counted them over and over.

❧

In a dark kitchen, my ears still burning,
I'd dump the lilo, binoculars, almanac
and close the door on the flourishing mess
of Arabic and broken lines.

❧

Though she swears they're not identical
when I dropped her sister at the airport
my palms hurt as she spoke my name
and I bit my tongue back when I kissed her.

❧

Nowadays, having shrunk the sky
to a skull-sized planetarium
—all fairy-lights and yawning voice-overs—
I only stay up for novae, or comets.

❧

Some mornings I wake and fantasize
I've slipped into her husband's place
as he breathes at her back, sliding his tongue
through Fomalhaut and the Southern Cross.

Seed

Parenthood is no more than murder
by degrees, the classic martyr-
dom. All the old myths are true: I pushed him under,
scything his bollocks off, stealing his thunder.

Leaking cock or bodged withdrawal,
ruptured condom, month-long vigil—
it is I who just escape with my life.
My child is hunting me down like a thief.

An Elliptical Stylus

My uncle was beaming: "Aye, yer elliptical stylus—
fairly brings out a' the wee details."
Balanced at a fraction of an ounce
the fat cartridge sank down like a feather;
music billowed into three dimensions
as if we could have walked between the players.

My Dad, who could appreciate the difference,
went to Largs to buy an elliptical stylus
for our ancient, beat-up Philips turntable.
We had the guy in stitches: "You can't . . .
er . . . you'll have to *upgrade your equipment.*"
Still smirking, he sent us from the shop
with a box of needles, thick as carpet-tacks,
the only sort they made to fit our model.

(Supposing I'd been *his* son: let's eavesdrop
on "Fidelities," the poem I'm writing now:
*The day my father died, he showed me how
he'd prime the deck for optimum performance:
it's that lesson I recall—how he'd refine
the arm's weight, to leave the stylus balanced
somewhere between ellipsis and precision,
as I gently lower the sharp nib to the line
and wait for it to pick up the vibration
till it moves across the page, like a cardiograph . . .)*

We drove back slowly, as if we had a puncture;
my Dad trying not to blink, and that man's laugh
stuck in my head, which is where the story sticks,
and any attempt to cauterize this fable
with something axiomatic on the nature
of articulacy and inheritance,
since he can well afford to make his own
excuses, you your own interpretation.
But if you still insist on resonance—
I'd swing for him, and every other cunt
happy to let my father know his station,
which probably includes yourself. To be blunt.

Amnesia

I was, as they later confirmed, a very sick boy.
The star performer at the meeting-house,
my eyes rolled back to show the whites, my arms
outstretched in catatonic supplication
while I gibbered impeccably in the gorgeous tongues
of the aerial orders. On Tuesday nights, before
I hit the Mission, I'd nurse my little secret:
Blind Annie Spall, the dead evangelist
I'd found still dying in creditable squalor
above the fishmonger's in Rankine Street.
The room was ripe with gurry and old sweat;
from her socket in the greasy mattress, Annie
belted through hoarse chorus after chorus
while I prayed loudly, absently enlarging
the crater that I'd gouged in the soft plaster.
Her eyes had been put out before the war,
just in time to never see the daughter
with the hare-lip and the kilt of dirty dishtowels
who ran the brothel from the upstairs flat
and who'd chap to let me know my time was up,
then lead me down the dark hall, its zoo-smell,
her slippers peeling off the sticky lino.
At the door, I'd shush her quiet, pressing
my bus-fare earnestly into her hand.

Four years later. Picture me: drenched in patchouli,
strafed with hash-burns, casually arranged
on Susie's bed. Smouldering frangipani;
Dali's *The Persistence of Memory*;
pink silk loosely knotted round the lamp
to soften the light; a sheaf of Penguin Classics,
their spines all carefully broken in the middle;
a John Martyn album mumbling through the speakers.
One hand was jacked up her skirt, the other trailing
over the cool wall behind the headboard
where I found the hole in the plaster again.
The room stopped like a lift; Sue went on talking.
It was a nightmare, Don. We had to gut the place.

The Alexandrian Library

Nothing is ever lost; things only become irretrievable.
What is lost, then, is the method of their retrieval, and
what we rediscover is not the thing itself, but the
overgrown path, the secret staircase, the ancient sewer.
                                    —François Aussemain

The lights go up: you find yourself facing
the wrangle of metal outside the Great Terminus.
You are poised on the end of the platform, the word
on the tip of its tongue: *There!* you shout, spotting
two rails still in spasm; they flex and unflex
like the last eels alive in the bucket.

As the train slithers out, you hang from the guard's van
to watch the tracks flailing from under the wheels;
this is no silver clew you will pay out behind you.
A few landmarks sail past in the wrong permutation
before the train pulls the ground over its head
and goes rocketing into the dark.

The intricate snare-rolls converge to beat
a slow tattoo as you file past the stations
sealed up between wars, like family vaults;
though you make out the posters for Eye Salts and Bloater Paste
the nameplates have all been unscrewed from the walls,
but peeling the gaffa-tape back from the map
you uncover the names of decanonized saints
and football clubs, now long-extinct.
Hours later, the train slams into the open—
light booms through the carriage; the sky is so low
you instinctively duck. After a rough night
the sun thuds away in its bleary corona;
a slack river drags itself under the hills
where the sheep swarm like maggots. These were the battlegrounds
abandoned in laughter, the borders no more

than feebly disputed; a land with no history,
there being no victors to write it. You lean
from the window to use the last shot in the spool:
the print slinks out like a diseased tongue.
When the laminates clear, the margin of black
has already begun to encroach from the left.
You pass the closed theme-park, a blighted nine-holer,
the stadium built for a cancelled event
now host to less fair competition:
a smatter of gunfire pinks at your cheek
as it leans on the glass. Now the line curves
over pitheads and slagheaps, long towns with one street
where only the kirk strains much above ground-level.
A station draws up, and slots into place
to fill the whole train with its name: COWDENBEATH

You alight; then a sharp suck of air at your back
whips you round—no train, no tracks, no ballast . . .
only the sleepers are left undisturbed
and bed themselves into the weeds. You jump down
and walk to the end of the line, where the sleepers
go angling into the ground, one by one;
it takes twice as long to walk back, since you stand
on the disinterred arc of a gigantic millwheel,
a cog in the planet's own secret machinery.
When you finally catch up with the platform, no one
is waiting to tear up the ticket you've lost
and the buses are off, so you set out on foot
for the northernmost tip of a council estate,
the last Pictish enclave, where beaky degenerates
silently moon at the back of the shops
while girls with disastrous make-up and ringworm
stalk past with their heads down and arms folded.

19

You are drawn inside the stone mouth of a tenement
where a young woman, soaping it out on her knees,
watches you try the blue door by the bin-recess
before shaking her head, then nodding you over.
You walk on to the soft punch of alien cooking,
now confused, as she ushers you past the wrecked pay-phone,
the windowless box-room, the ghost of a door
in the partition-wall, and then into the kitchen
where the smell and the steam-driven clitter of pot-lids
sends you rushing out into the drying-green.
Before you, surrounded by twelve of the blue doors,
are thirteen allotments; you make for the one
claimed only by nettles and scrub, with few clues
to the previous owner (potsherds, an old purse, some rope),
then tie up the fence-gate and sit down to think.

Think:
the brain,
having worked itself
into huge furrows through aeons
of failure to recollect something important,
still hoarding the nut of the pineal eye
where, neglected, the soul has reverted to grit;
though you frantically pass a charge over and over
the calcified circuitry, nothing will take
so you lower yourself down the chain of command
till you locate the flaw: the synaptic lacuna
where the spark of your most-treasured memory
finally fails in the crossing
and sinks in the gap
like Leander.

In
the dark
of your anorak pocket
your lily hand flutters awake:
three inches of card have slipped down from your cuff
like a hustler's ace. Exposed to the light
your lost ticket turns itself into a business card:
Harry Sturgis: Remaindered and Second-Hand Books.
On the back is a street-map, criss-crossed by two arrows;
one points to the shop, and one to a complicated
bit in the corner, bearing the legend:
You Are Here.
               You are there, on the breast of MacPhailor Street,

in the Heart of the Land of the Beaverboard Curtains,
where the cassies are frying with drizzle.
About to turn back from the boarded-up address
you notice the gap in the palings, the steps,
and gingerly feed yourself into the basement
where a rain-sodden carton of slushy romances
has decomposed into one big one. You shove
at the unnumbered door; there is a short kerfuffle
as books topple over behind it.

Harry himself does not stir from the counter
where he humps his one huge eyebrow, plotting daggers
on the Spot the Ball comp. on the back of the *Herald*
(Brechin v Raith, March 15th,
Conditions: muddy. Attendance: 55).
A sign reads "No Browsin—Dont Waist Your Time, Ask";
the walls are so stap-full, they look on the brink
of disgorging their contents, delivering up

the death you so often have dreamed of.
To your left is a corridor, book-clogged, low-ceilinged;
a cheesy light clings to the concatenation
of friable bell-wire and 40W bulbs.
You edge past the stuffed thing on guard at the entrance
while burnt stour and mildew make grabs for your throat.

This is no disappointment—each title bears witness
to Harry's appalling librarianship:
The Story of Purfling; Living with Alzheimer's;
Mastering the Nursery Cannon; back issues
of *Button Collector, Dogfighter Monthly*
and *Spunk; Mad Triste; The Use of Leucotomy*
in the Treatment of Pre-Menstrual Stress;
16 RPM—a Selective Discography;
Diabetic Desserts All the Family Will Love;
Origamian specials—*The Scissor Debate;*
Urine—The Water of Life; The King's Gambit—
Play it to Win; The Al Bowlly Songbook;
Beyond Dance—New Adventures in Labanotation;
The Volapük Scout Manual; piles of old sick-notes,
unmarked exam papers, staff memoranda
on Portion Control, and risible stabs
at the Unified Field Theory, furtively mimeoed
in the janitor's office in playtime;
The Late Correspondence of Breece D'J Pancake
and *The Poems of Erich von Däniken.*
                                  You have arrived,
in a fashion to which you have paid no attention,
at this small diverticulum, its wittering striplight
a gangrenous purple at either extremity.
On a whim, you lift a few books from the shelf—

I am John's Prostate; *The Cardinal's Mistress*;
the Book Club edition of *Josephine Mützenbacher*;
A Seven-Day Thinking course; *You and Your Autoharp*
and *Steal This Book* (signed, some foxing of endpapers)
—exposing the layer below; this yields up
Stanyhurst's *Vergil* and Pye's *Analecta*
(uncut); *Lady Bumtickler's Revels*; the Bible
they quietly pulped when the proof-reader's shopping-list
turned up in Numbers, thanks to some dickhead
apprentice compositor. You wistfully leaf
through a spineless edition of poor Hartley Coleridge:
No hope have I to live a deathless name ...

Squeering hard into the hole you have made
a new seam grows visible, packed like anthracite;
you work out a grimoire in horrible waxpaper,
a lost Eddic cycle of febrile monotony,
Leechdom and Wortcunning; *Living with Alzheimer's*
and Tatwine's gigantic *Aenigmae Perarduae*,
the whole thing a triple acrostic, and scrawled
onto wine-splattered oak-tag in the infantile hand
of the biggest joke in the scriptorium.

A tongue of dust, tasting of naphtha and pollen,
creeps out from the little vault, licking your hand
as it swims to the back and starts faking around;
from the scrips and the ashes you manage to fish out
a short monograph on the storage of turnips,
two bloodstained scytalae (wound round your arm
they read something about reinforcements); the Gospel
According to Someone Who Once Shagged the Sister
of St James the Less; Chaldean star-charts

mistaken for blotter, glutted with star-showers
and fat supernovae; The Lost Book of Jasher,
who could barely predict his own lunchtime.
Lastly, two scrolls trundle out to present themselves;
the name on the tag leaves you gasping for air:

φρυνιχος

       Divine Phrynicus, Lost Lord of Lost Hope,
of whom almost nothing survives but reports
of his greatness; Phrynicus, whose plays stuffed *Medea*
into third place in the Tragedy Contests,
one of them leaving the crowd so distressed
the authorities punished the man for his hubris.
But as you read on, your jaw falls even further
as you learn the real reason they fined him . . .
Mercifully, only the first act of *Battus,*
though *Myndon,* in all its woeful entirety,
unfurls to the floor with no flourish of trumpets
but a strangled toot, forlorn and wanky
like something some arsehole might blow in your face
at the end of a terrible party.

Wearily, you bury your arm to the shoulder,
your fingers at last touching stone; but your fingertips
go scuttling blindly across the clay prisms,
tracing the fugitive spoor of cuneiform
while you helplessly mouth the grim stories it tells,
the vowels shifting back down your throat as the language
grows cruder and cruder, turning the air blue.
Now, in the ur-bark your voice has become,
reputations deflate, heroes dwindle, till finally
when Helen revealed as a fifteen-stone catamite,
the Epic of Gilgamesh edited down

to the original camping-weekend, and *Yahweh*
just the noise that they made when the chisel slipped,
you swallow your tongue, and gag on the silence.
Your fingers rest on a great brass ring,
blissfully free from inscription; you stroke it
for comfort, and draw its dull glint through the dark,
so soothed by its light it takes seconds to register
the huge head on the end of it.

When your brain catches up with your legs, the damage
is already done, and every new turning
only compounds the original error;
slowing down to think, you only bring closer
the stamping and snorting behind you.
(How many times in the past has this horror
sent down, or sent up from the Dream below Dreams,
turned up in the whorehouse, the hospital corridor,
the laundrette, the lift or the school-dinner queue
to ferret you out of the dream-warren?
How many times have you found yourself scrabbling
up through the fathoms of earth, to emerge
nose-first from the turndown, your heart like a fist
at the trap you have only just bolted behind you?
And remember: in this world, as well as the real one,
none of the real doors are marked with big arrows.)
Going into a skid on the blindest of corners
you trip on a pile of misprinted erratum slips
and fly into space: landing, your fall
is conveniently broken by the full print-run
of *Gems of the Muse,* Vol. 9 (Buckfast Books);
and rifling through the top copy, you find it—
there, in the third line of *What is Emotion?*

by *Linda*—a misplaced full stop starts to spin,
then expands like a dead junkie's pupil, engulfing
the page, your hands, then your wrists, arms and torso,
the beast at your back, and the rest of it.

This is
Planck-Time
Absolute Zero
Albedo Fuck-All:
Luna Obscura, the old shunting-yard
where the dreams float to rest on their silent buffers.
Falling in with the zombified denizens (like them,
you imagine yourself quite alone) you begin
the nightly migration from Mare Incuborum
to Mare Insomniae, dustbowl to dustbowl,
ashpit to ashpit, your whole body polarized
by the rising meniscus, its cold incandescence
slitting your eyes with its light.

A sickle of moonlight
rests on the curve of her hip.
Through the net curtains, one night short of full,
the ancient bull-roarer hums low in the sky.
Your dearest one shifts in her sleep to lie facing you,
two tiny white moons in her wide-open eyes
and the wrong voice in her mouth:

So with one bound, Jack was free . . .
and he woke up to find it had all been a dream.
But when do you wake from the book of the dream,
shrug it off with a cold shower, a shot of black coffee?
There can be no forgetting; even after the fire
the archives are always somewhere intact—
in the world, or that part of the mind that the mind
cannot contemplate. But you have forgotten
the book you brought back; it lies on your pillow
as real as the pennies the tooth-fairies bring
or the horse's head left by the heavy squad.
Don't open it—the pages look blank in this light,
and tomorrow the words will draw your pen through them
until you have traced the whole terrible story
and think it your own. But no one man can own
a library book, and this library book
is already long overdue; hand it back—
there will be no tart letters or final demands,
just a knock at the door where no door ever was.

And you listen:
but it is only the milk-train

or your heart,
pounding over the points.

Next to Nothing

The platform clock stuck on the golden section:
ten to three. A frozen sun. The dead
acoustic of a small county; a dog-bark
is a short tear in the sky, above the wood.
The fixed stars crowd below the jagged awning.

Over the tracks, the ghost of the lame porter
stabs a brush along the ground, then vanishes.
The clock puts on a minute, tips the balance

and the stars fall as dust; birdsong thaws in the air.
The recorded voice addresses its own echo.

The Trans-Siberian Express

for Eva

One day we will make our perfect journey—
the great train smashing through Dundee, Brooklyn
and off into the endless tundra,
the earth flattening out before us.

I follow your continuous arrival,
shedding veil after veil after veil—
the automatic doors wincing away
while you stagger back from the buffet

slopping *Laphroaig* and decent coffee
until you face me from that long enfilade
of glass, stretched to vanishing point
like facing mirrors, a lifetime of days.

Pioneer

It's here I would have come to pass away
the final hour before the boat's departure;
the bluff side of the Law, between the harbour
and the dark, cetacean barrow of Balgay.

Twin trains of headlights inched across the river—
the homebound day-shift—trail-blazing cars
like angels on the starry escalator
of the bridge's tapering, foreshortened spar.

I tried to see it as a burning lance
angling for the slicked, black shoals of Fife
or a bowsprit, swung and steeved against the south

to help ride out her hellish afterlife:
the stubborn, rammish sap still on my hands,
the taste of her, like a coin laid in my mouth.

Wind-Tunnel

Sometimes, in autumn, the doors between the days
fall open; in any other season
this would be a dangerous mediumship
though now there is just the small exchange of air
as from one room to another. A street
becomes a faint biography: you walk
through a breath of sweetpea, pipesmoke, an old perfume.

But one morning, the voices carry from everywhere:
from the first door and the last, two whistling draughts
zero in with such unholy dispatch
you do not scorch the sheets, or wake your wife.

Poem

after Ladislav Skala

The ship pitched in the rough sea
and I could bear it no longer
so I closed my eyes
and imagined myself on a ship
in a rough sea-crossing.

The woman rose up below me
and I could bear it no longer
so I closed my eyes
and imagined myself making love
to the very same woman.

When I came into the world
I closed my eyes
and imagined my own birth.
Still
I have not opened my eyes to this world.

Perigee

Freak alignments. I am the best man,
she, the bridesmaid. John, the resident MC,
once our playground quarry, does not complain
when we corner him, frisking for his master key.

Our affair was stripped of all the usual padding—
just a flat joke about not getting "committed"
and a serviceable number by Joan Armatrading—
but we honed the *ruse de guerre* that first outwitted,
then destroyed our partners. I'd do sentry duty,
she, the dangerous stuff—who wouldn't trust her?

Posted at the door, I watch her spike
the marriage bed with handfuls of confetti,
discreet as fallout. Smiling, she swings back
towards me again, a natural disaster.

Bedfellows

An inch or so above the bed
    the yellow blindspot hovers
where the last incumbent's greasy head
    has worn away the flowers

Every night I have to rest
    my head in his dead halo;
I feel his heart tick in my wrist;
    then, below the pillow,

his suffocated voice resumes
    its dreary innuendo:
there are other ways to leave the room
    than the door and the window

Nil Nil

Just as any truly accurate representation of a particular geog-
raphy can only exist on a scale of 1:1 (imagine the vast, rustling
map of Burgundy, say, settling over it like a freshly-starched
sheet!) so it is with all our abandoned histories, those ignoble
lines of succession that end in neither triumph nor disaster, but
merely plunge on into deeper and deeper obscurity; only in the
infinite ghost-libraries of the imagination—their only possible
analogue—can their ends be pursued, the dull and terrible
facts finally authenticated.

—François Aussemain

From the top, then, the zenith, the silent footage:
McGrandle, majestic in ankle-length shorts,
his golden hair shorn to an open book, sprinting
the length of the park for the long hoick forward,
his balletic toe-poke nearly bursting the roof
of the net; a shaky pan to the Erskine St End
where a plague of grey bonnets falls out of the clouds.
But ours is a game of two halves, and this game
the semi they went on to lose; from here
it's all down, from the First to the foot of the Second,
McGrandle, Visocchi and Spankie detaching
like bubbles to speed the descent into pitch-sharing,
pay-cuts, pawned silver, the Highland Division,
the absolute sitters ballooned over open goals,
the dismal nutmegs, the scores so obscene
no respectable journal will print them; though one day
Farquhar's spectacular bicycle-kick
will earn him a name-check in Monday's obituaries.
Besides the one setback—the spell of giant-killing
in the Cup (Lochee Violet, then Aberdeen Bon Accord,
the deadlock with Lochee Harp finally broken
by Farquhar's own-goal in the replay)
nothing inhibits the fifty-year slide
into Sunday League, big tartan flasks,

open hatchbacks parked squint behind goal-nets,
the half-time satsuma, the dog on the pitch,
then the Boy's Club, sponsored by Skelly Assurance,
then Skelly Dry Cleaners, then nobody;
stud-harrowed pitches with one-in-five inclines,
grim fathers and perverts with Old English Sheepdogs
lining the touch, moaning softly.
Now the unrefereed thirty-a-sides,
terrified fat boys with callipers minding
four jackets on infinite, notional fields;
ten years of dwindling, half-hearted kickabouts
leaves two little boys—Alastair Watt,
who answers to "Forty," and wee Horace Madden,
so smelly the air seems to quiver above him—
playing desperate two-touch with a bald tennis ball
in the hour before lighting-up time.
Alastair cheats, and goes off with the ball
leaving wee Horace to hack up a stone
and dribble it home in the rain;
past the stopped swings, the dead shanty-town
of allotments, the black shell of Skelly Dry Cleaners
and into his cul-de-sac, where, accidentally,
he neatly back-heels it straight into the gutter
then tries to swank off like he meant it.

Unknown to him, it is all that remains
of a lone fighter-pilot, who, returning at dawn
to find Leuchars was not where he'd left it,
took time out to watch the Sidlaws unsheath
from their great black tarpaulin, the haar burn off Tayport
and Venus melt into Carnoustie, igniting
the shoreline; no wind, not a cloud in the sky
and no one around to admire the discretion
of his unscheduled exit: the engine plopped out
and would not re-engage, sending him silently
twirling away like an ash-key,
his attempt to bail out only partly successful,
yesterday having been April the 1st—
the ripcord unleashing a flurry of socks
like a sackful of doves rendered up to the heavens
in private irenicon. He caught up with the plane
on the ground, just at the instant the tank blew
and made nothing of him, save for his fillings,
his tackets, his lucky half-crown and his gallstone,
now anchored between the steel bars of a stank
that looks to be biting the bullet on this one.

In short, this is where you get off, reader;
I'll continue alone, on foot, in the failing light,
following the trail as it steadily fades
into road-repairs, birdsong, the weather, nirvana,
the plot thinning down to a point so refined
not even the angels could dance on it. Goodbye.

God's Gift to Women

❧

Prologue

A poem is a little church, remember,
you, its congregation, I, its cantor;

so please, no flash, no necking in the pew,
or snorting just to let your neighbour know

you get the clever stuff, or eyeing the watch,
or rustling the wee poke of butterscotch

you'd brought to charm the sour edge off the sermon.
Be upstanding. Now: let us raise the fucking *tone*.

Today, from this holy place of heightened speech,
we will join the berry-bus in its approach

to that sunless pit of rancour and alarm
where language finds its least prestigious form.

Fear not: this is spiritual transport,
albeit the less elevated sort;

while the coach will limp towards its final stage
beyond the snowy graveyard of the page,

no one will leave the premises. In hell
the tingle-test is inapplicable,

though the sensitives among you may discern
the secondary symptoms; light sweats, heartburn,

that sad thrill in the soft part of the instep
as you crane your neck to size up the long drop.

In the meantime, we will pass round the Big Plate
and should it come back slightly underweight

you will learn the meaning of the Silent Collection,
for our roof leaks, and the organ lacks conviction.

My little church is neither high nor broad,
so get your heads down. Let us pray. Oh God

00:00: Law Tunnel

leased to the Scottish Mushroom Company after its closure in 1927

(i)

In the airy lull
between the wars
they cut the rails
and closed the doors

on the stalled freight:
crate on crate
of blood and earth—
the shallow berth

of the innocents,
their long room
stale and tense
with the same dream

(ii)

Strewn among
the ragged queue—
the snoring king
and his retinue,

Fenrir, Pol Pot,
Captain Oates
and the leprechauns—
are the teeth, the bones

and begging-cup
of the drunken piper.
The rats boiled up
below the sleepers

(iii)

The crippled boy
of Hamelin
pounds away
at the locked mountain

waist-deep in thorn
and all forlorn,
he tries to force
the buried doors

I will go to my mother
and sing of my shame
I will grow up to father
the race of the lame

The Scale of Intensity

1) Not felt. Smoke still rises vertically. In sensitive individuals, déjà vu, mild amnesia. Sea like a mirror.

2) Detected by persons at rest or favourably placed, i.e. in upper floors, hammocks, cathedrals, etc. Leaves rustle.

3) Light sleepers wake. Glasses chink. Hairpins, paperclips display slight magnetic properties. Irritability. Vibration like passing of light trucks.

4) Small bells ring. Small increase in surface tension and viscosity of certain liquids. Domestic violence. Furniture overturned.

5) Heavy sleepers wake. Pendulum clocks stop. Public demonstrations. Large flags fly. Vibration like passing of heavy trucks.

6) Large bells ring. Bookburning. Aurora visible in daylight hours. Unprovoked assaults on strangers. Glassware broken. Loose tiles fly from roof.

7) Weak chimneys broken off at roofline. Waves on small ponds, water turbid with mud. Unprovoked assaults on neighbours. Large static charges built up on windows, mirrors, television screens.

8) Perceptible increase in weight of stationary objects: books, cups, pens heavy to lift. Fall of stucco and some masonry. Systematic rape of women and young girls. Sand craters. Cracks in wet ground.

9) Small trees uprooted. Bathwater drains in reverse vortex. Wholesale slaughter of religious and ethnic minorities. Conspicuous cracks in ground. Damage to reservoirs and underground pipelines.

10) Large trees uprooted. Measurable tide in puddles, teacups, etc. Torture and rape of small children. Irreparable damage to foundations. Rails bend. Sand shifts horizontally on beaches.

11) Standing impossible. Widespread self-mutilation. Corposant visible on pylons, lampposts, metal railings. Waves seen on ground surface. Most bridges destroyed.

12) Damage total. Movement of hour hand perceptible. Large rock masses displaced. Sea white.

The Chartres of Gowrie

for T. H.

Late August, say the records, when the gowk-storm
shook itself out from a wisp of cloud
and sent them flying, their coats over their heads.
When every back was turned, the thunder-egg
thumped down in an empty barley-field.

No witness, then, and so we must imagine
everything—from the tiny crystal-stack,
its tingling light-code, the clear ripple of tines,
the shell snapping awake, the black rock
blooming through its heart like boiling tar,

to the great organ of dawn thundering away
half-a-mile up in the roof, still driving
each stone limb to its own extremity
and still unmanned, though if we find this hard
we may posit the autistic elder brother

of Maurice Duruflé or Messiaen.
Whatever, the reality is this:
at Errol, Grange, Longforgan, and St Madoes
they stand dumb in their doorframes, all agog
at the black ship moored in the sea of corn.

11:00: Baldovan

Base Camp. Horizontal sleet. Two small boys
have raised the steel flag of the 20 terminus:

me and Ross Mudie are going up the Hilltown
for the first time ever on our own.

I'm weighing up my spending power: the shillings,
tanners, black pennies, florins with bald kings,

the cold blazonry of a half-crown, threepenny bits
like thick cogs, making them chank together in my pockets.

I plan to buy comics,
sweeties, and magic tricks.

However, I am obscurely worried, as usual,
over matters of procedure, the protocol of travel,

and keep asking Ross the same questions:
where we should sit, when to pull the bell, even

if we have enough money for the fare,
whispering *Are ye sure? Are ye sure?*

I cannot know the little good it will do me;
the bus will let us down in another country

with the wrong streets and streets that suddenly forget
their names at crossroads or in building-sites

and where no one will have heard of the sweets we ask for
and the man will shake the coins from our fists onto the counter

---

and call for his wife to come through, come through and see this
and if we ever make it home again, the bus

will draw into the charred wreck of itself
and we will enter the land at the point we left off

only our voices sound funny and all the houses are gone
and the rain tastes like kelly and black waves fold in

very slowly at the foot of Macalpine Road
and our sisters and mothers are fifty years dead.

A Private Bottling

So I will go, then. I would rather grieve over your absence
than over you.

—Antonio Porchia

Back in the same room that an hour ago
we had led, lamp by lamp, into the darkness
I sit down and turn the radio on low
as the last girl on the planet still awake
reads a dedication to the ships
and puts on a recording of the ocean.

I carefully arrange a chain of nips
in a big fairy-ring; in each square glass
the tincture of a failed geography,
its dwindled burns and woodlands, whin-fires, heather,
the sklent of its wind and its salty rain,
the love-worn habits of its working-folk,
the waveform of their speech, and by extension
how they sing, make love, or take a joke.

So I have a good nose for this sort of thing.

Then I will suffer kiss after fierce kiss
letting their gold tongues slide along my tongue
as each gives up, in turn, its little song
of the patient years in glass and sherry-oak,
the shy negotiations with the sea,
air and earth, the trick of how the peat-smoke
was shut inside it, like a black thought.
Tonight I toast her with the extinct malts
of Ardlussa, Ladyburn and Dalintober
and an ancient pledge of passionate indifference:
Ochon o do dhóigh mé mo chlairsach ar a shon,
wishing her health, as I might wish her weather.

When the circle is closed and I have drunk myself sober
I will tilt the blinds a few degrees, and watch
the dawn grow in a glass of liver-salts,
wait for the birds, the milk-float's sweet nothings,
then slip back to the bed where she lies curled,
replace the live egg of her burning ass
gently, in the cold nest of my lap,
as dead to her as she is to the world.

Here we are again; it is precisely
twelve, fifteen, thirty years down the road
and one turn higher up the spiral chamber
that separates the burnt ale and dark grains
of what I know, from what I can remember.
Now each glass holds its micro-episode
in permanent suspension, like a movie-frame
on acetate, until it plays again,
revivified by a suave connoisseurship
that deepens in the silence and the dark
to something like an infinite sensitivity.
This is no romantic fantasy: my father
used to know a man who'd taste the sea,
then leave his nets strung out along the bay
because there were no fish in it that day.
Everything is in everything else. It is a matter
of attunement, as once, through the hiss and backwash,
I steered the dial into the voice of God
slightly to the left of Hilversum,
half-drowned by some big, blurry waltz
the way some stars obscure their dwarf companions
for centuries, till someone thinks to look.

In the same way, I can isolate the feints
of feminine effluvia, carrion, shite,
those rogues and toxins only introduced
to give the composition a little weight
as rough harmonics do the violin-note
or Pluto, Cheiron and the lesser saints
might do to our lives, for all you know.
(By Christ, you would recognise their absence
as anyone would testify, having sunk
a glass of *North British,* run off a patent still
in some sleet-hammered satellite of Edinburgh:
a bleak spirit, no amount of caramel
could sweeten or disguise, its after-effect
somewhere between a blanket-bath and a sad wank.
There is, no doubt, a bar in Lothian
where it is sworn upon and swallowed neat
by furloughed riggers and the Special Police,
men who hate the company of women.)

O whiskies of Long Island and Provence!
This little number catches at the throat
but is all sweetness in the finish: my tongue trips
first through burning brake-fluid, then nicotine,
pastis, *Diorissimo* and wet grass;
another is silk sleeves and lip-service
with a kick like a smacked face in a train-station;
another, the light charge and the trace of zinc
tap-water picks up at the moon's eclipse.
You will know the time I mean by this.

Because your singular absence, in your absence,
has bred hard, tonight I take the waters
with the whole clan: our faceless ushers, bridesmaids,
our four Shelties, three now ghosts of ghosts;
our douce sons and our lovely loudmouthed daughters
who will, by this late hour, be fully grown,
perhaps with unborn children of their own.
So finally, let me propose a toast:
not to love, or life, or real feeling,
but to their sentimental residue;
to your sweet memory, but not to you.

The sun will close its circle in the sky
before I close my own, and drain the purely
offertory glass that tastes of nothing
but silence, burnt dust on the valves, and whisky.

To Cut It Short

a companion piece

And here is the great train three years later
hirpling into Vladivostok Central.
We may infer, from its caterwauling,
its sugared windows and scorched livery,
the grievous excess of its final night.

In a dub a half-mile up the track
nearby her upturned hostess trolley
lies the headless body of Scheherezade
whose stories would not tally; besides
I had heard the last already.

Buggery

At round about four months or so
—the time is getting shorter—
I look down as the face below
goes sliding underwater

and though I know it's over with
and she is miles from me
I stay a while to mine the earth
for what was lost at sea

as if the faces of the drowned
might turn up in the harrow:
hold me when I hold you down
and plough the lonely furrow

God's Gift to Women

Dundee, and the Magdalen Green.
The moon is staring down the sun;
one last white javelin inches out
of Lucklawhill, and quietly floats
to JFK or Reykjavik.
Newport comes on with a click
like the door-light from an opened fridge.
The coal train shivers on the bridge.

The east wind blows into his fist;
the bare banks rise up, thigh and breast;
half-blue, cursing under her breath,
the muddy Venus of the Firth
lunges through the waterburn.
You come: I wish the wind would turn
so your face would stay like this,
your lips drawn up to blow a kiss

even now, at your martyrdom—
the window, loose inside its frame,
rolls like a drum, but at the last
gives out, and you give up the ghost.
Meanwhile, our vernacular
Atlantis slides below the stars:
My Lord's Bank, Carthagena, Flisk
go one by one into the dusk.

So here we lie, babes in the wood
of voluntary orphanhood,
left in the dark to bleat and shiver
in my leaf-pattern duvet-cover,
and where Jakob of Wilhem ought to
stencil in the fatal motto
your bandage has unscrolled above
our tousled heads. Still, we survive—

although, for years, the doctors led
us back along the trail of bread
as if it ran to our rebirth,
not our stepmother's frozen hearth;
when they'd gone, she'd take us back
with big rocks in our haversacks
and twice as far in as before.
But I keep coming back for more,

and every second Wednesday
rehearse the aetiology
of this, my current all-time low
at twenty-seven quid a throw.
Ten years drawing out the sting
have ascertained the following:
a model of precocity—
Christ at one year, Cain at three

(a single blow was all it took;
the fucker died inside a week)—
I'd wed my mother long before
she'd think to lock the bathroom door,
as much a sly move to defraud
my father of his fatherhood
as clear the blood-debt with the gift
of my right hand; with my left

I dealt myself the whole estate
and in the same stroke, wiped the slate
of my own inheritance. Anyway,
as the semi-bastard progeny
of a morganatic union
(the Mother ranks below the Son)
I am the first man and the last:
there will be no title or bequest.

Once, to my own disbelief,
I almost took a second wife,
and came so close that others slurred
our names together as one word,
a word she gave, a word I took,
a word she conjured with, and broke.
So I filled the diary up again
with the absences of other men:

John's overtime, Jack's training-course,
returning in the tiny hours
with my head clear as a bullet-hole
and a Durex wrapped in toilet roll,
the operation so risk-free
I'd take my own seed home with me
and bury it deep down in the trash,
beside the bad fruit and the ash.

Thus the cross laid on my shoulder
grew light, as I grew harder, colder,
and in each subsequent affair
became the cross that others bear.
Until last night, when I found pain
enough to fill the stony grain
with that old yearly hurt, as if
I might yet burst back into leaf—

O my dear, my "delicate cutter"
pale phlebotomist, blood-letter—
the back of one, I came home drunk
to find you standing at the sink,
the steady eye of your own storm
feathering up your white forearm
with the edge of a Bic Ladyshave
and the nonchalance of a Chinese chef—

next month, when the scars have gone,
we'll raid the bank and hit the town,
you in that black silk dress, cut low
enough to show an inch or so
of the opalescent hand-long scar
on your left breast. Your mother swore
that fumbling along the shelf,
you'd pulled the pan down on yourself;

but we could see her tipping out
the kettle in the carry-cot,
one eyebrow arched above your cries
as she watched the string of blisters rise
to the design that in ten years
would mark you her inferior,
when all it did was make the one
more lovely than its own dear twin,

as if some angel'd shot his come
as bright as lit magnesium
across your body as you slept.
And as you lie here, tightly happed
in the track-marked arms of Morpheus,
I only wish that I could wish
you more than luck as you delay
before that white-gloved croupier

who offers you the fanned-out pack:
a face-card. The fey and sleekit jack.
The frame yawns to a living-room.
Slim Whitman warbles through the hum
of a bad earth. The Green Lady cries
over the scene: you, compromised,
steadily drawing out the juice
of the one man you could not seduce,

but his legs are sliding up his shorts,
his mouth drops open in its slot
and at the point you suss his groans
come not from his throat, but your own,
it all goes monochrome, and segues
into the usual territory.
You get up from your knees, nineteen,
half-pissed, bleeding through your jeans.

Titless, doll-eyed, party-frocked,
your mother, ashen with the shock
at this, the regular outrage,
pretends to phone the orphanage,
gets out your blue valise, and packs
it tight with pants and ankle-socks
and a pony-book to pass the time
on the long ride to the Home.

And then the old routine: frogmarched
outside to the freezing porch,
you'd shiver out the hour until
she'd shout you in and make the call;
but in your dreams they always come,
the four huge whitecoats, masked and dumb
with their biros, clipboards and pink slips,
the little gibbet of the drip,

the quilted coat with one long arm,
the napkin soaked in chloroform,
the gag, the needle and the van
that fires you down the endless lane
that ends in mile-high chicken-wire
around the silent compound, where
a tower-guard rolls a searchlight beam
over the crematorium—

Enough. Let's hold you in your dream,
leave the radio-alarm
mid-digit and unreadable,
under the bare bulb in the hall
one cranefly braced against the air,
the rain stalled like a chandelier
above the roof, the moon sandbanked
in Gemini. I have to think.

Now. Let us carefully assay
that lost soteriology
which holds Christ died to free himself,
or who slays the dragon or the wolf
on the stage of his presexual
rescue fantasy, makes the kill
not just for her flushed gratitude
but for his Father in the gods:

somewhere between His lofty blessing
and the virgin bride's undressing
the light streams from the gates of heaven
and all is promised and forgiven.
Time and again I blow the dust
off this wee psychodrama, just
a new face in the victim's role—
convinced if I can save her soul

I'll save my own. It doesn't work.
Whatever difference I make
to anyone by daylight is
dispatched in that last torpid kiss
at the darkening crossroads; from there
they go back to their torturers.
But if I could put the sleep I lose
over you to better use,

I'd work the nights as a signalman
to your bad dreams, wait for that drawn-
sword sound and the blue wheelsparks,
then make the switch before the track
flicks left, and curves away to hell . . .
This once I can, and so I will.
The death-camp gates are swinging to
to let you leave, not swallow you.

They set you down upon a hill.
Your case is huge. Your hands are small.
The sun opens its golden eye
into the blue room of the sky.
A black mare nods up to your side. You
take her reins, and let her guide you
over the sky-blue, trackless heather
to the hearth, the Home, your real mother.

The Lover

after Propertius

Poor mortals, with your horoscopes and blood-tests—
what hope is there for you? Even if the plane
lands you safely, why should you not return
to your home in flames or ruins, your wife absconded,
the children blind and dying in their cots?
Even sitting quiet in a locked room
the perils are infinite and unforeseeable.
Only the lover walks upon the earth
careless of what the fates prepare for him:

so you step out at the lights, almost as if
you half-know that today you are the special one.
The woman in the windshield lifting away
her frozen cry, a white mask on a stick,
reveals herself as grey-eyed Atropos;
the sun leaves like a rocket; the sky goes out;
the road floods and widens; on the distant kerb
the lost souls groan and mew like sad trombones;
the ambulance glides up with its black sail—

when somewhere in the other world, she fills
your name full of her breath again, and at once
you float to your feet: the dark rose on your shirt
folds itself away, and you slip back
into the crowd, who, being merely human,
must remember nothing of this incident.
Just one flea-ridden dog chained to the railings,
who might be Cerberus, or patient Argos,
looks on, knowing the great law you have flouted.

Imperial

Is it normal to get this wet? Baby, I'm frightened—
I covered her mouth with my own;
she lay in my arms till the storm-window brightened
and stood at our heads like a stone

After months of jaw jaw, determined that neither
win ground, or be handed the edge,
we gave ourselves up, one to the other
like prisoners over a bridge

and no trade was ever so fair or so tender;
so where was the flaw in the plan,
the night we lay down on the flag of surrender
and woke on the flag of Japan

Little Corona

i.m. Radka Toneff

C:... true, but there is, however, often a real event which triggers what Jabès called our "endocrine fantasies." For example, there was a boy in our village, Goran ... I don't recall his last name, but his family were from way up on the Ukraine border ... who played peckhorn or euphonium with the local marching band, and had the most extraordinary skill: he was able to get a tune out of almost anything, and could make a whistle from a piece of macaroni, a zither from a cigarette packet ... Once, I remember, he had us all spellbound as he blew the guts from a goose-egg, and then fashioned a kind of primitive ocarina, and on this absurdly delicate instrument blew a strange little off-key melody, almost more breath than note ... I hear it clearly in the lochrian mode of so many of the folk-songs of the region, but this is too convenient to be more than a trick of memory ...Then this scrawny Orpheus, as soon as he knew we were all drawn into his magic, crushed it in his hand, as if out of pure scorn for us; this trick would always draw an involuntary groan from his audience, and the first time I witnessed it I burst into tears ... the sudden, immaculate, irrevocable disappearance of both the singer and the song seemed such a terrifying thing ... I can still see his terrible grin ...

from *Armonie Pierduta şi Regăsita: Emil Cioran*, reprinted in *The Aquarian*, no. 12/13, trans. Tess DiMilo

12:00: Dronley

August 20th, 1998, and when I say *Dronley,* I mean more
specifically 351/366 on OS *Pathfinder* map 338. Meet me in
the deciduous part of the forest, but take the east approach,
via Bridgefoot and Templelands. Remember, if God's huge
hand were to descend from the clouds or the clear skies,
straying indolently over these rough forestry pines, they
would feel to him as the pale down on your arm does to me
now; whereas the tiny blood-tick that negotiates it—look—
rears and tilts like a landrover. When I was two or three, I
used to wake up in tears because my parents had such empty
faces . . . the two lonely eyes, the solitary mouth . . . Many
years later, I met a man who explained this to me. Most of us
have fallen here. (A few—a merciful few—have climbed.) As
every adolescent uniquely observes, it's all infinitely relative,
then; but a *point* can still exist, the notional singularity from
which we can take our bearings, and know how late or how
early, or from how far or how high, we have come. So we will
talk, or will have talked, in what we will think is silence,
deepening and deepening as, one by one, the machines—
hitherto unnoticed by us—shut down: the hay-bailer in the
next field; the distant traffic from the city; the earth's own
secret engines, and then all the clockwork of the heavens, our
words suddenly free in the air, as if they were solid print, then
statues, then angels.

The Alexandrian Library
Part II: The Return of the Book

For M.D.
the bigger fibber

Before I set pen to paper, a preparative: I close my eyes and
imagine myself in another library, where I am sitting with my
eyes closed, imagining myself in this one. Being, like most men,
far more impressed by the simulacral than the procession of
shabby realia with which we are daily confronted (it being only
in the former that we ever truly rejoice in the hand of the cre-
ator), upon opening my eyes again I affect a genuine astonish-
ment at the pathologically detailed universe my imagination
has brought into being. Of course I have done nothing more
than return the world to the world again, which is the same as
rendering it to God, or whatever deranged Caesar happens to
be holding the reins today...
                                        —François Aussemain

The level blue gaze of the lovely librarian
has wrestled your own to the floor,
half-an-hour of her husky insistence finally
coaxing from you, like a long-buried skelf,
the real reason you can't seem to talk to your father.
Beneath the professional concern, you detect
something akin to desire;
though she must let you work, now, and leaves
with a quick little squeeze of the shoulder,
sexually neutral, but somehow prolonged enough
not to oblige you to write off the much-refined
after-hours stockroom scenario
as wishful thinking entirely.
You keep listening, till the bristling efficiency
of her nylons criss-crossing inside her starched whites
has shushed the whole place back to silence.

The tip of your ballpoint is weeping black ink
over the snowy divan of the notepad,
as if it were dreaming incontinently
of the glories to come, but this is the real thing,
and as such it will get the full treatment:
the thirty-seven classical stations of courtly love,
the hymeneal rites of Byzantine complexity,
the Song and the Book and the Film of the Act,
its magnification, discussion, rehearsal,
its almost-indefinite postponement:
for no one has had this idea before—
how you will cherish their tear-stricken faces
the morning you fly the stained sheets from the window!

While shifting your weight to one buttock, silently
breaking the seal on an odourless fart,
you split open the vacuum of black Costa Rica;
the smell of it, capric, deeply provocative,
swims up and wafts itself under your nose
like a flick-knife. You refresh your favourite mug,
the blue Smarties job with the handle still on.
The ghost of your hangover thunders away
(like a train; this should go without saying)
into the featureless steppes, its heart set
on magnetic north; in a couple of hours
it will dock in a small town just short of the Circle,
known dimly, if anyone knows it at all,
for its lead-mines, a dangerous method of throat-singing
and an ardent liqueur, distilled from white turnips
with the taste and appearance of liquid acetylene
and its consequent, utterly perfect effacement
of perceptual borders; two fingers of this stuff

and everything turns into everything else.
At midnight, you tattoo the Horseman's Word
on the back of your wrist with a pin and a biro,
then slip into blissful insentience.
In the morning, excluding the state of your trousers,
it seems there's no damage to pay;
just a stunned vacuity, furred at the edges,
as if you looked out at the world through a big hole
someone had smashed in your living-room window.
A little confused, you spend an hour failing
to scrub the word SPONG from your wrist, then set out
for a leisurely tour of the second-hand book-stalls.
Around midday, you notice the demon of accidie
perched on the steeple, yawning contagiously;
you make plans to deal with him, considering, in turn,
a propitiatory nap, the dubbed Polish game-show,
even, roguishly, the hair of the dog.
On the last stroke of noon, he lets fly with the ice-pick
you will wear in your head for a fortnight.

You've developed the habit, at this hour, of randomly
lifting a book from the shelves;
here, there are nothing but books about Art,
that is to say, books with just pictures;
Monday was Twombly, yesterday Watteau,
this afternoon, Balthus: brought to the light,
the brilliant plan you have unconsciously nursed
for the past fifteen minutes turns out to be merely
the prospect of having a wank before teatime.
You will swither luxuriously over a choice:
to swan up, or not, to the top of the building,
then the one extra flight to the glassy enclosure

you share with the brown-winged, probationary angels,
to settle back under the skylight, with Balthus
spread out on the tiles, while the pine-scented ozone
comes walloping in through the vent.
(An atom-sized blowfly goes zipping erratically
across the white field of your conscience, too small
for conclusive identification.)

In the stillness, you make out the delicate jangle
of tiny chimes, thin rods of crystal and amethyst
threaded on silk; to play them, it strikes you,
would feel just like stroking a feather;
it is a universe, advanced in its state
of chromatic decay, gently disbanding
in the long pole of sunlight that falls from the ceiling,
fixing your jotter exactly. Right now,
if literature were quantum mechanics
you'd be just a sniff from the theory of everything—
one breezy reckoning on the back of a beermat
and that would be that, bugger Einstein. As it is,
with the silence now thickened enough to be workable
and the words ranged like tools on an infinite shadow-board,
each one on the tip of your tongue (i.e. *ranine*),
it is almost time to begin.

The library is losing all faith in itself
—a good sign, you know—as if seconds before
the wall had sprung back from the floor like a pop-up book
to be fingered by God, his hand bracing your shoulder
to steady you as he yanks at the tab
that sticks out of your head, making your writing arm
jerk up and down in big squiggles.

———

Now everything hangs in the balance,
as if the whole world could be brought into being
by the fact of its clear elocution, as if
the planet now hovered and hummed on the brink
of the great bimillennial switch of polarities
that wiped out the dinosaurs, kick-started the ice-age,
knocked up the virgin, and in the next hour
will deflect the moon out of its course.

Now the last touch: your new toy, *"Infraworlds—*
For the Gentle Enhancement of Personal Space,"
a series of ambient soundtracks designed
to be superimposed over absolute silence,
since virtually nothing is on them.
You have *Scottish Renaissance, Café Voltaire*
and *Library,* though, as usual, you plump for
Buenos Aires, Early Evening, 1899,
firk out the cassette from its soft pastel cover
and jiggle it into your Walkman.
At first, there seems to be nothing but tape-hiss
though it seeps imperceptibly into the white rush
of steam from a kettle of maté;
through the half-opened casement, a spatter of horse-traffic,
the shudders and yawns of a distant bandoneon;
from a bar on the opposite side of the street,
over the blink of small glasses, two men
discuss metaphysics, or literature;
from previous listenings you know, in an hour or so,
the talk will come round to the subject of women,
and then to one girl in particular;
and end with the phthisical freshing of metal
(you will whack up the volume for this bit),

a short protestation that ends in a gurgle,
the screak of a chair-leg on ironwood parquet
and your man spanking off down an alley.
Till then, you will work.

The new poem is coming along like a dream:
this is the big one, the one that will finally
consolidate everything. It is the usual,
but different: a series of localized, badly-lit,
paradigmatic atrocities seen
from a train at the hour between dusk and oblivion,
but—O his audacity!—rendered as *pastoral*:
the sensitive, paranoid, derelict romance,
the only response that is humanly adequate
now, at this point at the end of the century;
the song that the rest will all find themselves singing
too late, and the words will be yours. You will sue.
It is perfect in length, while your witless coevals,
all keen, when the big flash goes off, to be caught
in the apposite gesture, have spent the last five years
conscientiously failing to finish the epic
or grinding and polishing four lines of nothing
in the desperate hope that the planet will somehow
fall into its transparent curves.

In the poem you appear as a poet, a real one,
with a book out, and two or three gigs in the diary
though neither the taxman, your shrink nor the Gas Board
is having it. Last week, at the manse
for the cosy wee pep-talk arranged by your mother,
the minister, somewhere between the sweet sherry
and the meat-paste and cucumber sandwiches

leant across, laid his fat paw on your shoulder
and whispered *For fuck's sake, get real, son.*
The train in the poem is rushing you home
as if it remembered what you had forgotten
to water or feed or lock up or turn off;
perhaps you will find the whole house has been stolen,
in its place, just the transom you failed to snib shut;
and what parcel of bloodsuckers, slugs and winged beetles
will the late second post have chucked up on the doormat—
the summons, the X-ray results, the week's notice
of the warranty sale, the genuine death threats
from the jealous, the recently badly-reviewed,
the nutter you met at the workshop?
Now enter the bit-player you think you remember
from the black-and-white Carry-On films, though in your poems
invariably cast as the louche psychopomp—
widow's peak, wall-eye, BO, the lot.
A full set of obsolete dental equipment
fills his breast-pocket; trailing a fingertip
over the tight row of flame-burs and stylets
he pauses over a mildew-pocked speculum
with which he will take all the time in the world
to find everything wrong with your ticket.
You are describing his hand falling down on your shoulder
    like something to do with a hawk or a lobster
        when his hand falls down on your shoulder
            in precisely the manner you failed to describe,
            and somehow the big switch is made.

The lens flies back, offering a view
of yourself from above, then the two of you, stiff
in a caption of light, the last in a series
of bright rooms, some empty, some spartanly furnished
with their little vignette, like an unfinished strip-cartoon
of which you are clearly the punchline;
then plunges away through the abstracted night
till the train is no more than the pulsating hyphen
in London–Brighton, a jittery point
of no ascertainable hue or dimension
that resolves as the glint in his good eye,
has a half-hearted stab at a twinkle, then fails.
And there, on the page, is the lovely librarian,
the coffee so vividly drawn you could smell it
were it not for the audible whine of his oxters,
his skidmarks and forty years' Kensitas
that admits of no other alternative.

॰

They have let you go home. You sit in the dark,
count slowly up to fifty,
then switch on that absolute moron, the anglepoise:
with a sputter of wet wood, the back of your head
explodes in slow motion; through the axehead of sparks
come the horror-waves no one has ever conveyed
without buggering with the typography:
your writing is almost entirely illegible,
and you will never know, since you cannot remember
whether you'd sat in the train or the library,
if it was the page, or your hand shaking.

ENVOI

Someone appears to be using your mouth
to scream through: you shut it abruptly,
oddly relieved to discover the neighbours
pounding the wall, in concern or annoyance;
unfortunately, your house is semi-detached,

that is the gable-end, this is the first floor,
    and, with a bang and a fizz,
here is a door where no door was before
    and where the door was no door is

19:00: Auchterhouse

My pulse clicks in my throat, so hard it hurts.
The Sunshine Coach will never break through, stalled
forever on its sad trawl of the schemes,
each rain-dark tenement surrendering up
its palest child. Laid out for little games,
the big house waits with us: one student nurse
and one fourteen-year-old, his forage cap
ablaze with badges: *First Aid*; *Hygiene*; *Fire Drill*.

Gail is lightly braced against the sink,
her face burning, her skirt bunched round her middle
while I try to effect the painless removal
of the inch-long skelf, buried in her flank.
I will not be disturbed; this is heart surgery,
and might well take me an eternity.

from Advice to Young Husbands

No one slips into the same woman twice:
heaven is the innocence of its beholding.

From stroke to stroke, we exchange one bliss
wholly for another. Imagine the unfolding
river-lotus, how it duplicates
the singular perfection of itself
through the packed bud of its billion petticoats,
and your cock, here, the rapt and silent witness,
as disbelief flowers from his disbelief.

Heaven is the innocence of its beholding:
no man slips into the same woman twice.

Candlebird*

after Abbas Ibn Al-Ahnaf, c. 750

If, tonight, she scorns me for my song,
You may be sure of this: within the year
Another man will say this verse to her
And she will yield to him for its sad sweetness.

'*"Then I am like the candlebird,"*' he'll continue,
After explaining what a candlebird is,
'*"Whose lifeless eyes see nothing and see all,*
Lighting their small room with my burning tongue;

His shadow rears above hers on the wall
As hour by hour, I pass into the air."
Take my hand. Now tell me: flesh or tallow?
Which I am tonight, I leave to you.'

So take my hand and tell me, flesh or tallow.
Which man I am tonight I leave to you.

*Generic name for several species of seabird, the flesh of which
is so saturated in oil the whole bird can be threaded with a wick
and burnt entire.

The Eyes

versions after Antonio Machado

❧

Advice

My advice? To watch, and wait for the tide to turn—
wait as the beached boat waits, without a thought
for either its own waiting, or departure.
As I put it so well myself: "The patient triumph
since life is long, and art merely a toy."

Well—okay—supposing life is short,
and the sea never touches your little boat—
just wait, and watch, and wait, for art is long;
whatever. To be quite honest with you,
none of this is terribly important.

To Emiliano Barral

Plane by plane,
corner by corner,
your chisel struck upon me
holding my breath
in the frozen dawn
of this porphyry block,
or at least the man I now
want in my mirror:
the Spanish Buddha, in all
his idle grandeur!
The dumb, slaked mouth,
the ears set to the wall
of silence, and under
the bare slope of the brow,
eyes scooped from the rock—
from rock, that I might not see.

The Eyes

When his beloved died
he decided to grow old
and shut himself inside
the empty house, alone
with his memories of her
and the big sunny mirror
where she'd fixed her hair.
This great block of gold
he hoarded like a miser,
thinking here, at least,
he'd lock away the past,
keep one thing intact.

But around the first anniversary,
he began to wonder, to his horror,
about her eyes: *Were they brown or black,*
or grey? Green? Christ! I can't say . . .

One Spring morning, something gave in him;
shouldering his twin grief like a cross,
he shut the front door, turned into the street
and had walked just ten yards, when, from a dark close,
he caught a flash of eyes. He lowered his hat-brim
and walked on . . . *yes, they were like that; like that . . .*

Profession of Faith

God is not the sea, but of its nature:
He scatters like the moonlight on the water
or appears on the horizon like a sail.
The sea is where He wakes, or sinks to dreams.
He made the sea, and like the clouds and storms
is born of it, over and over. Thus the Creator
finds himself revived by his own creature:
he thrives on the same spirit he exhales.

I'll make you Lord, as you made me, restore
the soul you gifted me; in time, uncover
your name in my own. Let that pure source
that pours its empty heart out to us pour
through my heart too; and let the turbid river
of every heartless faith dry up for ever.

Meditation

Is my heart asleep?
Has the dream-hive
fallen still,
the wheel that drives
the mind's red mill
slowed and slowed
to a stop, each scoop
full of only shadow?

No, my heart's awake,
perfectly awake;
it watches the horizon
for the white sail, listens
along the shoreline
of the ancient silence

Paradoxes

(i)

Just as the lover's sky is bluest
the poet's muse is his alone;
the dead verse and its readership
have lives and muses of their own.
The poem we think we have *made up*
may still turn out to be our truest.

(ii)

Only in our sorrows do we live
within the heart of consciousness, the lie.
Meeting his master crying in the road,
a student took Solon to task: "But why,
your son long in the ground, do you still grieve—
if, as you say, man's tears avail him nothing?"
"Young friend," said Solon, lifting his old head,
"I weep *because* my tears avail me nothing."

Poetry

In the same way that the mindless diamond keeps
one spark of the planet's early fires
trapped forever in its net of ice,
it's not love's later heat that poetry holds,
but the atom of the love that drew it forth
from the silence: so if the bright coal of his love
begins to smoulder, the poet hears his voice
suddenly forced, like a bar-room singer's—boastful
with his own huge feeling, or drowned by violins;
but if it yields a steadier light, he knows
the pure verse, when it finally comes, will sound
like a mountain spring, anonymous and serene.

Beneath the blue oblivious sky, the water
sings of nothing, not your name, not mine.

Promethean

The traveller is the aggregate of the road.
In a walled garden beside the ocean's ear
he carries his whole journey on his coat—
the hoarfrost and the coffee-smell, the dry heat
of the hay, the dog-rose, the bitter woodsmoke.
The long day's veteran, he puts a brake
on all sentiment, and waits for the slow word
to surface in his mind, as if for air.

This was my dream—and then I dreamt that time,
that quiet assassin drawing us through the days
towards our end, was just another dream . . .
And at that, I saw the gentle traveller lift
his palm to the low sun, and make a gift
of it: the Name, the Word, the ashless blaze.

Road

Traveller, your footprints are
the only path, the only track:
wayfarer, there is no way,
there is no map or Northern star,
just a blank page and a starless dark;
and should you turn round to admire
the distance that you've made today
the road will billow into dust.
No way on and no way back,
there is no way, my comrade: trust
your own quick step, the end's delay,
the vanished trail of your own wake,
wayfarer, sea-walker, Christ.

Siesta

Now that, halfway home, the fire-fish swims
between the cypress and that highest blue
into which the blind boy lately flew
in his white stone, and with the ivory poem
of the cicada ringing hollow in the elm,
let us praise the Lord—
the black print of his good hand!—who has declared
this silence in the pandemonium.

To the God of absence and of aftermath,
of the anchor in the sea, the brimming sea...
whose truant omnipresence sets us free
from this world, and firmly on the one true path,
with our cup of shadows overflowing, with
our hearts uplifted, heavy and half-starved,
let us honour Him who made the Void, and carved
these few words from the thin air of our faith.

3 O'Clock

The plaza and the blazing orange-trees,
    laden with fat suns.

Then chaos from the little school—
    the stiff air suddenly filled
        with shrieks and yells—

that wild joy
    in the corners of the dead cities!

And something we were yesterday
    that we discover still alive,
        like a river's pulse
            just below the ancient streets . . .

The Waterwheel

The evening is falling,
dusty and sad;
the millstream still mutters
its little work-song
in the slats and the scoops
of the slowing wheel;
the mule's drifting off
—poor old mule!—
as the shadows grow long
in the sound of the water.

What divine poet
blindfolded you,
my wretched old pal,
and tied the perpetual
wheel to the water's
mindless soliloquy,
I can't say, but know this:
his was a heart
ripened in darkness
and slowed with knowledge.

The Work

My heart was where a hundred dusty roads
crossed and then ran on; or it was a station
full of hopeful travellers, though not one
had either lodgings or a real appointment.
Whatever it was—my heart, within a day,
was scattered on a hundred winds, and sped
through canyons, deserts, river-plains and valleys
to dark ports, sea-lanes, unmapped continents.

But now, like a swarm returning to the hive
at that purple hour when all the crows go hoarse
and sail off to the crags and the black eaves,
my heart turns to its melancholy work
with nectar gathered from a hundred flowers
and the hundred sorrows of the gathering dark.

To the Great Zero

When the *I Am That I Am* made nothingness
and, as He deserved, went back to sleep—
day had night, and man companionship
in woman's absence. He was bored to death.
Fiat Umbra! And on that godless Sabbath
man laid his first thought: the cosmic egg,
chill and pale and filled with weightless fog,
hovered like a face before his face.

The zero integral, that empty sphere:
only when our heads are in the air
is it ours. So now the beast is on his feet
and the miracle of non-being complete—
let's rise, and make this toast: a border-song
to forgetting, amnesty, oblivion.

New Poems

The Wreck

But what lovers we were, what lovers,
even when it was all over—

the bull-black, deadweight wines that we swung
towards each other rang and rang

like bells of blood, our own great hearts.
We slung the drunk boat out of port

and watched our sober unreal life
unmoor, a continent of grief;

the candlelight strange on our faces
like the tiny silent blazes

and coruscations of its wars.
We blew them out and took the stairs

into the night for the night's work,
stripped off in the timbered dark,

gently hooked each other on
like aqualungs, and thundered down

to mine our lovely secret wreck.
We surfaced later, breathless, back

to back, and made our way alone
up the mined beach of the dawn.

Luing

When the day comes, as the day surely must,
when it is asked of you, and you refuse
to take that lover's wound again, that cup
of emptiness that is our one completion,

I'd say go here, maybe, to our unsung
innermost isle: Hirta's antithesis,
yet still with its own tiny stubborn anthem,
its yellow milkwort and its stunted kye.

Leaving the motherland by a two-car raft,
the littlest of the fleet, you cross the minch
to find yourself, if anything, now deeper
in her arms than ever—sharing her breath,

watching the red vans sliding silently
between her hills. In such intimate exile,
who'd believe the burn behind the house
the straitened ocean written on the map?

Here, beside the fordable Atlantic,
reborn into a secret candidacy,
the fontanelles reopen one by one
in the palms, then the breastbone and brow,

aching at the shearwater's wail, the rowan
that falls beyond all seasons. One morning
you hover on the threshold, knowing for certain
the first touch of the light will finish you.

St. Brides: Sea-Mail

Now they have gone
we are sunk, believe me.
Their scentless oil, so volatile
it only took one stray breath on its skin
to set it up—it was our sole
export, our currency
and catholicon.

There was a gland
below each wing, a duct
four inches or so down the throat;
though it was tiresome milking them by hand
given the rumour of their infinite
supply, and the blunt fact
of our demand.

After the cull
we'd save the carcasses,
bind the feet and fan the wings,
sew their lips up, empty out their skulls
and carry them away to hang
in one of the drying-houses,
twelve to a pole.

By Michaelmas,
they'd be so light and stiff
you could lift one up by its ankle
or snap the feathers from its back like glass.
Where their eyes had been were inkwells.
We took them to the cliffs
and made our choice.

Launching them,
the trick was to "make
a little angel": ring- and fore-
fingers tucked away, pinkie and thumb
spread wide for balance, your
middle finger hooked
under the sternum.

Our sporting myths:
the windless, perfect day
McNicol threw beyond the stac;
how, ten years on, Macfarlane met his death
to a loopback. Whatever our luck,
by sunset, they'd fill the bay
like burnt moths.

The last morning
we shuffled out for parliament
their rock was empty, and the sky clear
of every wren and fulmar and whitewing.
The wind has been so weak all year
I post this more in testament
than hope or warning.

My Love

It's not the lover that we love, but love
itself, love as in nothing, as in O;
love is the lover's coin, a coin of no country,
hence: the ring; hence: the moon—
no wonder that empty circle so often figures
in our intimate dark, our skin-trade,
that commerce so furious we often think
love's something we share; but we're always wrong.

When our lover mercifully departs
and lets us get back to the business of love again,
either we'll slip it inside us like the host,
or beat its gibbous drum that the whole world
might know who has it. Which was always more *my* style:

O the moon's a bodhran, a skin gong
torn from the hide of Capricorn,
and many's the time I'd lift it from its high peg,
grip it to my side, tight as a gun,
and whip the life out of it, just for the joy
of that huge heart under my ribs again.
A thousand blows I showered like meteors
down on that sweet-spot over Mare Imbrium,
where I could make it sing its name over and over.
While I have the moon, I wailed, *no ship will sink,*
or woman bleed, or man lose his mind;
but reader, I was terrible—
the idiot at the session spoiling it,
as they say, for everyone.
O *kings* petitioned me to pack it in.

The last time, I peeled off my shirt
to find a coffee bruise from hip to wrist
and two years passed before a soul could touch me.

Even in its lowest coin, it kills us to keep love,
kills us to give it away; all of which
brings me to Camille Flammarion,
signing the flyleaf of his *Terres du Ciel*
for a girl down from the sanatorium,
and his remark—the one he couldn't *help* but make—
on the gorgeous candid pallor of her shoulders;
then two years later, unwrapping the same book,
reinscribed in her clear hand, *with my love,*
and bound in her own lunar vellum.

The White Lie

I have never opened a book in my life,
made love to a woman, picked up a knife,
taken a drink, caught the first train
or walked beyond the last house in the lane.

Nor could I put a name to my own face.
Everything we know to be the case
draws its signal colour off the sight
till what falls into that intellectual night

we tunnel into this view or another
falls as we have fallen. *Blessed Mother,*
when I stand between the sunlit and the sun
make me glass: and one night I looked down

to find the girl look up at me and through
me with such a radiant wonder, you
could not read it as a compliment
and so seek to return it; in the event

I let us both down, failing to display
more than a half-hearted opacity.
She turned her face from me, and the light stalled
between us like a sheet, a door, a wall.

But consider this: that when we leave the room,
the chair, the bookend or the picture-frame
we had frozen by desire or spent desire
is reconsumed in its estranging fire

such that, if we slipped back by a road
too long asleep to feel our human tread

we would not recognise a thing by name,
but think ourselves in Akhenaten's tomb.

Then, as things ourselves, we would have learnt
we are the source, not the conducting element.
Imagine your shadow burning off the page
as the dear world and the dead word disengage—

in our detachment we would surely offer
such offence to that Love that will suffer
no wholly isolated soul within
its sphere, it would blast straight through our skin

just as the day would flush out the rogue spark
it found still holding to its private dark.
But like our ever-present, all-wise god
incapable of movement or of thought,

no one at one with all the universe
can touch one thing; in such supreme divorce
what earthly use are we to our lost brother
if we must stay partly lost to find each other?

Only by this—this shrewd obliquity
of speech, the broken word and the white lie,
do we check ourselves, as we might halt the sun
one degree from the meridian

then wedge it by the thickness of the book
that everything might keep the blackedged look
of things, and that there might be time enough
to die in, dark to read by, distance to love.

DON PATERSON was born in Dundee in 1963, and works as a writer, editor, and musician. His poetry collections are *Nil Nil*, *God's Gift to Women*, and *The Eyes*. He has also edited *101 Sonnets*, a selected Robert Burns, and (with Jo Shapcott) *Last Words*. He has been the recipient of several literary awards, among them the T. S. Eliot Prize, the Geoffrey Faber Memorial Award, the Forward Prize for Best First Collection, and three Scottish Arts Council Book Awards. He is currently Poetry Editor for Picador. As well as poetry, he writes drama for the stage and for radio, and has worked as a reviewer and columnist for several national newspapers; he currently reviews computer games for the *Times*. As a jazz guitarist, he works solo with the ensemble Lammas, which he co-leads with the saxophonist Tim Garland, and with whom he has recorded five albums; the most recent of these is *Sea Changes*. He has also composed for the classical instrument. Having lived in London for many years, he now divides his time between Edinburgh and Kirriemuir. He is presently working on a fourth collection, a version of Rilke's *Sonnets to Orpheus*, and a book on poetic composition.

The text in this book has been set in Janson, a typeface based on the original work of Miklós Kis, a Hungarian typographer who spent most of the 1680s in Amsterdam and was a major figure in Dutch typography. For many years Kis's work was incorrectly ascribed to the Dutch punchcutter Anton Janson. This book has been designed by Wendy Holdman, set in type by Stanton Publication Services, Inc., and manufactured by Hignell Book Printing on acid-free paper.

Graywolf Press is a not-for-profit, independent press. The books we publish include poetry, literary fiction, essays, and cultural criticism. We are less interested in best-sellers than in talented writers who display a freshness of voice coupled with a distinct vision. We believe these are the very qualities essential to shape a vital and diverse culture.

Thankfully, many of our readers feel the same way. They have shown this through their desire to buy books by Graywolf writers; they have told us this themselves through their e-mail notes and at author events; and they have reinforced their commitment by contributing financial support, in small amounts and in large amounts, and joining the "Friends of Graywolf."

If you enjoyed this book and wish to learn more about Graywolf Press, we invite you to ask your bookseller or librarian about further Graywolf titles; or to contact us for a free catalog; or to visit our award-winning web site that features information about our forthcoming books.

We would also like to invite you to consider joining the hundreds of individuals who are already "Friends of Graywolf" by contributing to our membership program. Individual donations of any size are significant to us: they tell us that you believe that the kind of publishing we do *matters*. Our web site gives you many more details about the benefits you will enjoy as a "Friend of Graywolf"; but if you do not have online access, we urge you to contact us for a copy of our membership brochure.

www.graywolfpress.org

Graywolf Press
2402 University Avenue, Suite 203
Saint Paul, MN 55114
Phone: (651) 641-0077
Fax: (651) 641-0036
E-mail: wolves@graywolfpress.org